DREAM MAP (WISH MAP)

Detailed manufacturing guide. Feng Shui - We Attract Wellbeing

Alex Magic

CONTENTS

INTRODUCTION

Why Create A Wish Map

It may seem that this book fell into your hands by accident. It is unlikely that this is really so, because such important events, if they happen by chance, then very rarely. It is much more likely that you are now holding instructions on how to make amazing changes in your life for the better. If you remember the circumstances that led you to the meeting with the book, then surely a lot will seem strange.

There is really nothing to be surprised at - this is how the World works and synchronicity manifests itself. Whether to read this instruction, whether to use it - decide for yourself. In my firm conviction, even this question cannot be - of course, you need to use it!

It is very likely that you have never heard of the Card, and in this regard, many questions arise: what is the Card of Desires, why is it needed? Why waste your time and create your own Map? How does it work and why can it really help fulfill your dreams?

The fact is that you and I live in a rather interesting time. Every day more and more people begin to feel and understand that in addition to the familiar physical reality, there is a huge invisible World that can influence people, help them, or vice versa. That there are forces of enormous power that affect not only individuals, but entire planets and even galaxies.

These forces can be called in different ways, as someone is more familiar with: the World, the Universe, the Absolute, Spirit, higher Forces, the Universe, Space, God ... the terms are not so important here. Personally, I love the word Peace, and, with your permission, I will use it on the pages of the book.

For thousands of years, mankind has tried to learn the secrets of these Forces, to learn how to use their power for its own benefit. Of course, such knowledge has always been secret, and therefore was passed only from initiate to initiate. But in the last two or three decades, a real breakthrough has occurred, and this knowledge is slowly becoming available to us. You can see this for yourself by the huge amount of literature that has filled the book shelves. Why is this happening? Because there are already quite a large number of people who have begun to think about the World, their place in it and their interaction with it. Sometimes they say about such people "they woke up", and personally I really like this phrase.

Let me compliment you. Once for some reason you have taken this book in your hands, it means that you too "Wake up". Congratulations! It's great!

So, if there are Forces capable of controlling global processes, then it seems obvious that it will not be difficult for them to fulfill our desires at all. Do you know what is most wonderful? This is that they are happy to help us. You will ask why? Because when we go to our light and good goals, we ourselves become better, and when we become better, then the whole World becomes better. More kindness, light, love, joy and happiness appear. When we change, the whole vast World changes for the better together with us, no matter how strange it may seem.

But that's not all. It turns out that everyone is a magician to some extent, without even knowing it. Inside each of us there is a piece of the great possibilities of the World, so we also have a powerful force with which we can shape events, manage our destiny, live the life of our dreams and achieve goals.

This is hard to believe, so people are driven from yourself away from the thought that they are potential wizards and everything is in their hands. It is easier for them to think that something external is to blame for all their difficulties and problems - from a bad boss to their own unhappy Destiny, from which they cannot escape, as it seems to them. Let's tell you a secret, people do not have Destiny in the sense that there is no one clear plan according to which we go from birth to death, without being able to deviate from someone's program. We are not robots doing our program blindly. We are human. And we came to this World for a reason ... We came for experience, lessons and soul development. Our life is hundreds and thousands of predetermined variants of Destiny, among which there are such wonderful ones that we have never even dreamed of. And it's up to us to decide which option we go for - better or worse. Once a person understands that he created all his problems himself, as soon as he takes responsibility for everything that happens to him, real magic begins. And if he thinks that he is just a pawn in someone's hands and cannot influence anything, then with such thoughts he simply blocks the awakening of the wizard in himself. What do we end up with? First, we know that the World and the Universe are ready to help us. Secondly, we ourselves have a magical power from birth. Isn't that enough? we ourselves have a magical power from birth. Isn't that enough?

All this sounds very inspiring, but what does Kart have to do with it?

The fact is that it is she who acts as a kind of conductor between the World and us, informs him about what we want and what we need. If we have a correctly created Wish Card, then the World will definitely pay attention to us. Yes, the World is ready to help us, but in most cases the World simply does not hear us and does not even know what we need help. For the World to help, it must be asked correctly, and, unfortunately, not everyone can.

Since the Card is directly connected with the Subtle World, it itself uses enormous Powers and opportunities for our dreams to come true. Sometimes her own energy is enough for this.
And also the Wish Card activates our inner strength. When we create it, invest time and effort into it, we reveal our magical essence.

It turns out that those who create the Map receive the most powerful support from the World, become stronger, and even the Map itself helps them. Is not that great?

It is also remarkable that the Wish Card is one of the few techniques that helps in almost all areas of life, because it has its own division: wealth, career, creativity, health, love and more. This means that she is able not only to fulfill some one desire, like most techniques, but to change a person's whole life for the better: whatever you need, whatever you dreamed of, Karta is ready to help!

Just think - there is a tool for changing your whole life! Often a person allows himself to dream only of little things, such as a new car. And the Card can help change a whole life. This is fantastic!

That is why it is worth making a Wish Card. This is a truly magical tool with which you can create real miracles. And only you decide if you need this tool.

But definitely worth a try!

DREAM MAP APPEARANCE

The Dream Card is a very effective technique that combines not only the methods of wish fulfillment systems, but also the capabilities of various energy and information systems. As a result, she uses the Energies and possibilities of the surrounding World. Agree that this is just great! you can create a dream card with your own hands or online! Some people like to place a dream map on their desktop, but this is not always the right way. You can find out more on our website.

Visually, the Map most often looks like a square, divided into 9 equal-sized sectors of a strictly defined color. Less common are options in the form of an octagon or rectangle. Further, we will always consider exactly the square version.

These nine multicolored squares represent the skeleton of the Map. Nine squares are a fundamental feature of this technique and they make it easily recognizable. If you see 9 multi-colored squares of certain colors, then this is the Dream (Treasure) Card. If you see a sheet of paper undivided into squares, even with many images of desires in various areas of life, then this is a Dream Collage, not a Map.

Where did these 9 squares come from, and for some reason, certain colors? This division is based on the Ba Gua Eight Life Aspirations technique. Perhaps you know that there are Sectors responsible for certain areas of our life, the South is the Fame Sector, the North is the Career, the East is the Health, etc. Let us remind you right away that in Feng Shui, north and south change places, i.e. the south is at the top.

The colors of the squares are as follows:

south (central upper square) - red,
north (central lower) - blue,
west (right) - white
east (left) - green
southeast (upper left) - light green or light green,
southwest (upper right) brown,
northwest (lower right) - gray,
 northeast (lower left) - light brown,
central - yellow.

After the squares are painted in the desired colors, they become not just squares, but full-fledged parts of a magic tool, so from this moment we respectfully call them Sectors, with a capital letter!

The main difference between the Sectors is not at all in color. And the fact that each of them affects one or another area of the life of the creator of the Map. Therefore, in the Sector, they place images of what a person wants, and always together with his photo. In other words, in each Sector there are several (possibly one, of course) dream collages corresponding to this Sector.

Let's list all the Sectors:

The Southeast (upper left) Sector is one of the most important because it is responsible for wealth! Everything that you want to buy and everything related to finance is posted here.
The South (Upper) Sector is the Glory Sector. This Sector helps to achieve success and recognition in society.
Southwest (upper right) Sector - the zone of love, marriage, relationships.
The Western (right) Sector is the Children and Creativity Sector. Everything related to these aspects is posted here.

Caution, incorrect placement of images in this Sector can lead to unwanted pregnancies. More on this and more in the article on How to Make a Map .

Northwest (lower right Sector) symbolizes travel. In addition, it is also the Sector of Assistants and Mentors, therefore images of people whose help a person needs are placed here. You can also place here the image of your heavenly assistants, for example, angels.
The North (lower) Sector is everything related to a career.
The Northeast (bottom right) Sector is responsible for wisdom and knowledge.
East (left) Sector - Family and Health Sector.
Central Sector - main dreams, goals, desires. Which to place - you yourself must decide. If it is difficult to choose one dream, then post several.

Different authors have different interpretations about the Central Sector. Another variant of its use as the Health Sector is often found. Which option is correct? It was not easy for us to understand this at all, because both options have strong pros and cons. In the end, I had to ask for help from our Information Sources from the Subtle World. We got advice. Our Sources unambiguously consider the "Central Sector - main dreams, goals, desires" option to be more favorable and effective.

Location, colors and purpose of the Dream Map Sectors

The illustration below helps to quickly remember the location, color and responsibility of the Sectors.

Fig.1 Coloring scheme and assignment of the Dream Map Sectors

It remains to say about one more feature of this tool: in the general case, it is created only for a year.

Perhaps now you have some idea of what the Treasure Map looks like and what is in it. Of course, this information is absolutely insufficient. You have a long way to go to study it further, so that the actually created Map becomes truly magical. After all, almost everything is important in it: from the date of creation to the size and the choice of photos for collages. Start by reading all the materials on the site, this will quickly learn very important things. Most of them are the result of our own research over many years.

Do you think that you already know a lot about the Map? Do you want to test your knowledge? Below is one real Sector from the Dream Map of our friend - Alex the lion, which he sent us to check and find errors. We upset Alex a little by informing him that we found more than 10 bugs. How many mistakes will you notice?

HOW TO MAKE A MAP

As you know, the term Dream Card has several synonyms: Treasure Card, Desires, Feng Shui, Happiness, ... Personally, we like the Dream Card and Treasure Card option more. In the materials of the site, the words Map of Dreams, Map, Map of Dreams (Treasures) mean the same thing.

When deciding how to make a Dream (Treasure) Card, it is important to understand that it can be made in various designs. In this article, we will look at some of them in terms of achieving maximum efficiency.

The main variants of the Card are:
1. Large on the wall;
2. Small in the folder;
3. All Sectors separately;
4. Virtual.

So, let's consider each of the options in detail.

Option 1. Large Dream Map on the wall

The most common and effective option is the following: The card is inserted into a beautiful frame under glass and hangs on the wall in a specially selected place. The map is quite large, the length of the frame side is 50 - 60 - 70 centimeters or more, depending on the specific placement conditions, taking into account the favorable dimensions. This option is convenient to implement, because there is enough space to accommodate the necessary desires.

With such sizes, it is more convenient to work with photo collages located inside the Sectors, because there is no need to suffer by cutting out tiny images. Working with this option, it is much easier to take into account absolutely all our recommendations. The map will hang on the wall, constantly drawing your attention, so it is constantly activated, which is very good. This is the most efficient version of this technique.

But there are situations when this option cannot be used. If you live in a hostel or in a rented apartment, if people who are not very close to you can see this magical artifact, then you will have to think about another option.

Option 2. Small Dream Map in a folder

If you need to hide the Map from unwanted eyes, then it seems quite logical to decide to simply reduce its size so that it can be stored in some folder or album. It is quite possible to do this, but you need to be prepared for the appearance of many problems. We will list some of them.

The biggest challenge will be the lack of space. Judge for yourself: the width of an ordinary A4 sheet is 21 cm.This means that you can print a drawing with a width of about 20 cm on an ordinary printer. By the way, this is a very favorable size, but even more favorable sizes are in the range from 20.2 to 21 cm.

Then the size of each of the 9 Squares will be about 7 cm.Let's discard 0.5-1 cm from each side, which will be occupied by the edging of beads, and we will get a very small square with a side length of six centimeters, into which you need to fit your dreams, moreover, together with amplifiers. It is very likely that this size "will not be enough".

This is the main disadvantage of the second option. The plus is that it is possible to keep the Card away from prying eyes. You will place it, for example, in a folder with files, which you will view whenever you want.

Let's say right away that the problem of lack of space on a sheet of approximately 20 x 20 cm, it turns out, can be solved. We learned this method from our Information Sources, which constantly help us to understand the secrets of this unique technique. We tell about him, as well as about tens (or hundreds?) Of other secrets in our author's Course. After getting to know him, you will not have any questions about how to make the Map correctly and as efficiently as possible.

Option 3. All Sectors separately

Sometimes you can find the following advice on how to get by with A4 format to create a Map: arrange each of the nine Sectors on a separate A4 sheet, and then place all the sheets in the desired sequence in a file folder or album. It seems that the sheep will be safe and the wolves will be fed, because everything will easily fit into a regular folder with files, while the size of each Sector will be large enough.

Unfortunately, we cannot recommend using this option. The problem of separating the nine Sectors from each other, which may seem small to some, is actually huge. Our Sources believe that the effectiveness of the third option is tens (!) Times lower than the second.

Pay attention to this case. We just gave an example of how the efficiency of the Map can decrease if the recommendations for its creation are not followed. Just think, cut the Map into squares and put each of them on its own page. And what happened ?! What happened is that its magical structure was destroyed and as a result we have nine independent Collages of Dreams.

There are many other nuances, neglect of which can reduce the effectiveness of this magic tool by orders of magnitude. Do you need it? Many of our recommendations may seem strange, incomprehensible, insignificant, so there may be a desire to neglect some of them. But we assure you that every secret, every advice has been tried, checked and studied. They are all important. Therefore, our advice is not to try to decide for yourself what is important and what is not. If you make a Map, it is better to make it right. Don't risk your dreams!

Option 4. Virtual Dream Map on the computer screen

We have seen cases when people made their beautiful Dream (Treasure) Map in Photoshop and simply saved it on the computer. As a result, a virtual Map was obtained, which was constantly in front of our eyes and could be instantly removed from the screen when an outsider appeared.

We strongly recommend that you do not do this. The tool created by such a guide is unlikely to be able to effectively fulfill real desires. At least, our Sources very much doubt this. It must really exist so that it can be felt. At the same time, it is quite permissible to photograph your real Map and place this image on a computer so that you can look at it at any time.

So, the **best option** is a large framed Map hanging on the wall. If you need to hide your dreams from prying eyes, then the best option is to create one smaller Dream Card, consisting, as it should be, of 9 Squares. It seems to us that it is most convenient to use A4 sheets, because it is for it that folders with files are made.

HOW TO PREPARE
TO CREATE A MAP

As you know, the term Dream Card has several synonyms: Treasure Card, Desires, Feng Shui, Happiness, ... Personally, we like the Dream Card and Treasure Card options more. In the materials of the site, the words Map of Dreams, Map, Map of Dreams (Treasures) mean the same thing.

Before making a list of what needs to be prepared for making the Map with your own hands, you need to decide on the methods for creating it.

There are several ways:
- The map is manually created on a sheet of Whatman paper;
- The map is completely created in a graphics editor, for example, in Photoshop;
- a combination of the first and second options to one degree or another.

But there are also absolutely exclusive options. For example, you can draw it, but for that you need to be an artist. Or embroider with your own hand with all the patterns. We will talk about such methods separately, but for now we will discuss the methods that are most often used.

Ways to Create a Dream Map

Method 1. The map is manually created on a sheet of Whatman paper.

All 9 Sectors are manually painted over. Photo collages are created manually, i.e. they cut out their photographs with scissors and then stick them on the images of their dreams. Activators and amplifiers are glued by hand. The edging of Sectors from beads is added manually. Then everything is inserted into the frame.

Method 2. The map is completely created in a graphics editor, for example, in Photoshop.

In this case, it is more convenient to work not with a common Map file, but with nine separate files, each of which corresponds to one of the nine Sectors. In the editor, the squares are painted, all photo collages are created in it, and then activators and amplifiers are added. Next, you will need to print the created images of the Sectors, of course, it is much better to do this on a color printer. You can bring the finished files to an Internet cafe or computer club and print there. Just be sure to warn that you need well-defined image sizes. Then all that remains is to stick the printed sheets on whatman paper.

If you have access to a flatbed printer, you can print the entire Map and then stick it on a drawing paper. If the printer can only work with A4 sheets, then each Sector will have to be printed out separately, of course, also on photographic paper, and then cut out and carefully glued onto whatman paper in turn.

You can do without a Whatman paper, simply by connecting the Sectors on the back with scotch tape, but on a Whatman paper it will work out much better.

When printing, we strongly recommend using photo paper rather than regular office paper. Do not be afraid of this word, because 9 sheets of photo paper are very inexpensive, especially since matte photo paper, which is much cheaper, is quite suitable. The density of photographic paper is desirable in the region of 140-170 g / cm 2.

All that remains is to manually add a bead edging and insert the Card into the frame.

Method 3. This is a combination of the first and second options to one degree or another. More often they do this: Sectors on a Whatman paper are created manually - with paints. In a graphic editor, each of the many photo collages is created, and then they are printed on photo paper, cut out and manually pasted on the Dream Card with their own hands.

There are several options for coloring the Sectors:

• you can paint them with paint,
• you can use colored paper, cut out the Sectors of the required size from it and stick them on whatman paper
• you can print the Sectors of the desired color on a printer, and then cut them out and paste them on whatman paper.
• Recall that you can completely create a Map in a graphical editor, then you will print completely ready-made squares - both with filling and with content.

We have now listed only the main ways to create a Dream Map, exactly those that are available to most people. But there are absolutely exclusive options. For example, you can draw it, but for that you need to be an artist. Or embroider with your own hand with all the patterns. Of course, in such special cases it will be impossible to comply with all our recommendations, but we think that the tremendous effort spent on creating such cards will increase their power to enormous proportions.

THINGS TO PREPARE TO CREATE A DREAM MAP

So, to create a Map with your own hands you will need:

1. **Good scissors.** If you make photo collages by hand, you will have to cut out a lot of pretty small images and a lot of your beautiful heads. You don't want to cut off half of your face because of blunt scissors ...

2. **Whatman paper.** First, decide on the desired size of the Card, and then decide whether one sheet of Whatman paper will be enough for you. Recall that the size of an ordinary sheet of Whatman A1, which can be bought in a store, is 594 x 841 mm. Whether the width of 594 mm is enough for you or whether you have to buy two sheets and glue them end-to-end is up to you.

3. **Paints and a brush.** This is necessary for those who manually paint the Sectors. You already know the colors of all Sectors, so you understand what colors are needed. We only remind that the white Sector must also be colored.

Important! Someone may come up with an original idea to use not paints for coloring the Sectors, but felt-tip pens or pencils. Let's just say this is a bad idea. We specifically found this out.

Important! If you understand that for some unthinkable reason you will not be able to paint all 9 Sectors in the correct colors, then the only correct way out is this: paint everything in one color. A much worse option from the point of view of the further effectiveness of the **Dream Map** would be to paint over correctly some of the Sectors, and some - as necessary. Those. or paint all Sectors in the correct colors, or make all Sectors the same color.

4. **Images of your dreams.** Either in the form of pictures on the computer, or cut from magazines. In what specific form they are needed depends on the way in which you will make collages.

5. **Your photos** . Or in the form of pictures on a computer, or real ones. Which ones are needed depends on the way in which you will make collages.

6. **Glue** to glue photo collages or printed Sectors to whatman paper. It is better to use glue. Actually, for this it is much more convenient to use **double-sided tape** , then you will not risk accidentally smearing glue all over the Sector. The card does not like such bullying. But PVA is still needed to neatly glue the edging of the Sectors from beads.

7. **Beads in** nine colors to match the colors of the Sectors. Actually, beads are not a must at all. But using it to frame Sectors increases efficiency so much that we highly recommend using it.

8. **Frame with glass** . The frame is also optional, but it is so useful that we highly recommend using it as well.

We almost forgot to say about the most difficult and responsible part of preparing for the creation of a Treasure Map with our own hands: you definitely need to clearly define your desires and dreams. It is not at all as easy as many people think .

DREAM CARD.
PHOTO DESIRES

As you know, the term Dream Card has several synonyms: Treasure Card, Desires, Feng Shui, Happiness, ... Personally, we like the Dream Card and Treasure Card options more. In the materials of the site, the words Map of Dreams, Map, Map of Dreams (Treasures) mean the same thing.

There is no point in creating a Dream Map if you have not decided what should be shown on it. And sometimes it's not easy to decide. It only seems at first glance that everyone knows what he wants. In fact, most people without preparation can only say something like "I want to be rich." But in our case, specificity is required, but in "I want to be rich" there is no specificity. Is being rich getting twice as much as now? Or a thousand times more? How much to weigh in grams? Be sure to clearly define the goals, otherwise the Map will not know what the task is.

You don't need to think that you can formulate all desires, dreams, goals in just ten minutes. We assure you that after such a sprint decision, your magical assistant for a whole year will sooner grieve than please, because not those dreams that are actually important and desirable will be placed on her. It is much more correct to allocate enough time for this and calmly think about what you want. Let a few more days pass after that, during which you will recheck yourself many times: do I really want this? And only then will you be able to confidently say to yourself: "Yes, this is exactly what I want!"

There are several very important rules when determining desires and setting goals.

Rule: Desire must be real!

If you really want to buy a particular car model for yourself, and your husband persistently persuades you to choose another car, then it would be a great folly to post a collage with the car that your husband advises. The world will not do anything against your will and your desire. Therefore, Karta will simply refuse to work to fulfill this "false" desire.

You should not portray yourself against the background of the pyramids of Egypt just because a friend thinks this is the best vacation spot if you yourself have long dreamed of the delightful Adriatic Sea in Croatia.

You do not need to pretend to be admitted to a prestigious economic university (as your mother advises) if you dream of becoming a doctor.

There is no point in thinking about losing ten kilograms, if in fact, deep down, you like your own figure.

Why the above rule exists is quite understandable. It is impossible to deceive the World, because he perfectly understands where the real desire is, and where is the trick. Therefore, there is no point in wasting time and energy on posting a dream that is not really a dream. It will not come true!

Attention! Mir has a good sense of humor, and it is quite possible to assume that some of these "fake" desires may come true. Only it will not bring joy, only problems.

Much worse is that the presence of such a "fake" dream significantly reduces the likelihood of all other desires being fulfilled. Why does this happen? Because a properly created Map is not just a picture on the wall, but an almost magical tool with which the most cherished dreams can come true. And you need to treat this instrument appropriately - with respect and love. If we break this first rule, then we are showing clear disrespect for the Dream Card. It's no surprise that it can stop working altogether, turning from a powerful artifact into an ordinary picture on the wall.

Rule: Real but magical desires

Although the Dream (Treasure) Map is a magical tool, we strongly recommend that you place only real, not fantastic desires on it. Did this phrase upset you? In vain, because our understanding of the reality of a dream is somewhat different from the generally accepted one.

If you have never traveled outside your village and have a salary of $ 100, then can you dream of a vacation in Bali? Of course you can! In our opinion, this is a completely normal, real desire.

If you live in a hostel, would it be fantastic to want to become an apartment owner within a year?

No, it won't, because such things happen, so this is a very real dream.

If you have a project that requires a lot of money to implement, wouldn't it be fantastic to dream of its implementation? No, this is a very real desire, because the World can bring a project sponsor to you.

In these examples, you see that the rule of reality of desires does not in the least prevent the setting of seemingly unattainable goals.

But if a person has half a centner of excess weight, high blood pressure and shortness of breath, does not play sports at all, but dreams of flying into space for a year, then, from our point of view, this is a fantastic desire.

If someone runs 100 meters in 13 seconds and wants to become a world record holder in a year, then this is also a fantastic desire.

If a person has not written lines in his life, but dreams of becoming the author of a world bestseller in a year, then it looks like science fiction.

It is impossible to train your body in a year to drop 3 seconds in the 100m to a new world record. And it is hardly possible to become a world famous author in a year if there is no talent or at least abilities.

As you yourself understand, you should not load the Dream Card with tasks that it cannot complete without your hard work, despite the fact that you are not at all determined to get down to business seriously. For example, half a centner of excess weight will not go anywhere if their owner eats five Big Macs at night.

So, dream boldly, no need to limit yourself in desires. But be realistic wizards.

Rule: Allow yourself to dream big

We highly recommend that you allow yourself to choose such desires that would be greater than what you yourself consider possible.

For example, it is stupid to set the task of raising your salary by 10%, although you know from your work experience that you cannot even question 5% of your bosses. It is quite possible that the World has prepared for you options for income growth tenfold, and it will not necessarily be wages. And then you will block a much more monetary option with your 10% desire.

Allow yourself to swing at a more meaningful goal than what you think is possible at the moment. Do not limit the World in its desire to help you. But remember that dreams and desires must be real, i.e. though magical, but not entirely fantastic.

Rule: desires should be self-directed!

It is useless to wish a friend to finally have a family. Let her place this dream on her own Map. It makes no sense to place in your Card the desire for the son to go to college. This is your Card, not his. But you may well wish that your help to your son and maternal support would help him to enter. Do you feel the difference?

What to wish for in difficult Sectors

Another pleasant difficulty lies in wait for you - the absolute need to come up with goals and desires for the eight directions of your life. Why this can be a difficulty is understandable, but why enjoyable? Because the Card almost by force makes you remember that a harmonious person has not only material goals. There is also Love, good relationships, relaxation, creativity, recognition and so on.

Usually it is quite easy for a person to come up with wishes for the Wealth, Health and Family, Love, Travel and Helpers Sectors. There it is roughly clear what to wish for.

But what to have in the Glory Sector, for example? Should everyone dream of winning an Oscar? But this is clearly unrealistic!

Of course, it is impossible to include desires in the "difficult" Sectors just for show, so that there is something in them, yes. A Dream (Treasure) card may well take offense at such a frivolous attitude towards it. But the fear of these Sectors is completely in vain, because every normal person has something to wish for in them. Let's go over these Sectors.

Children and Creativity Sector

The part that concerns children is more understandable: if we dream of a child, then we post a photo of the baby here. If we do not want to have a child this year, we will not post it.

And what about creativity? Not everyone can create at the level of great composers and musicians, or write books. Of course, not everyone. But each person is engaged in creativity at home, at work, on vacation, often not noticing it. Someone wants to come up with the most delicious cake, someone dreams of coming up with a new way of processing parts, someone creates new computer programs, someone starts raising a child in a completely new way, someone creates their own website. All this creativity! And you said that there is nothing to include in this Sector ...

Glory Sector

We already said that it is not at all about getting an Oscar or constantly shining on TV screens. It is about recognizing your merits, experience, knowledge and skills. And this recognition can take place in the family, at work, in some kind of company or community.

Maybe your salads are considered the most delicious, and friends are happy to come to visit to enjoy them and praise the hostess. Maybe you play the guitar better than anyone in the company of tourists, and for this you are especially appreciated. Maybe you manage to cope with an almost insoluble problem at work, and the whole team applauds you for a long time. Or your Facebook page is gaining popularity before our eyes. Or maybe you are standing on the podium, breaking the world record or on the stage of a huge hall. Each has its own glory.

Agree that it is very difficult to live without recognition of your talents and skills from others. Do you want such recognition? Fill the Glory Sector!

Knowledge and Skills Sector

In fact, this is not a very difficult Sector, just many adults allow themselves to be lazy and do not want to learn something new.

Perhaps you are finally planning to learn to speak English fluently? Or learn a new programming language? Or take some training courses? Learn to work in Photoshop? Hand over to the right? New to downhill skiing? Learn extreme driving? Learn to edit your site yourself? Finally, learn how to make sure that the yolk does not spread in the fried eggs?

See how many things you can think of for this Sector!

Career Sector

Are you, like others, intimidated by the harsh word "Career"? Do you think that if you already have the highest rank or category, then there is nowhere to grow further? This is a completely wrong opinion!

A career is not only (and not so much) growth in the career ladder (higher position, category, category). This Sector contains those goals and dreams that can be defined as "doing more and better". For example, you are planning to increase your income from doing something. Either your company expands, or you take on more and more complex projects. Or maybe now you are one of several equivalent specialists, and you want to become the best. Or earlier you were entrusted with simpler tasks, and you want to learn how to solve the most difficult ones (with a corresponding increase in your income, of course). If you work in a network company, then a career is clearly understood to mean reaching some high level.

As you can see, there are no particular difficulties in these supposedly "difficult" Sectors. You just need to remember that creativity, recognition, new knowledge and personal development are also important for a versatile person.

PHOTOS AND PICTURES FOR TREASURE MAP

We have repeatedly said that desires and dreams in the Treasure Map are arranged in the form of collages, where the image of a dream is combined with a photograph of a person. The final efficiency of the Map greatly depends on whether the collages are made correctly. Unfortunately, unsuccessful photographs of a person and the image of his desire can "spoil" the collage.

Here are some tips for taking your photos to create a Treasure Map:

1. You should not use just one or two of your photos. Don't be greedy, take **more pictures!**

2. It is not at all necessary to be photographed in the studio. **Clear** amateur photos are also great .

3. It would be wrong to use your favorite photos from graduation, which took place 10 years ago. **Old photos are bad!**

4. Photos should be in **color** , they work much better.

5. Photos should be taken at a time when **you are in a good mood** . There is no point in trying to fake a forced smile while in a depressed mood. Energy cannot be fooled! Any image of a person preserves his energy and his emotions. If you were photographed in a bad mood, then the negative Energies that the photo will keep will interfere with the Card's work. And if you took pictures on a sad day - for example, your favorite hamster died on that day - then each time you look at the Treasure Map, you will remember your experiences that day. And instead of joyful Energies, you will radiate the pain of loss and sadness. This will also prevent the Card from working effectively.

6. Photos **must be free from defects** . Remember that the Treasure Map is an almost magical artifact. He perceives your desires exactly as they are stated, presented, depicted. And it is difficult to guess in advance what the Card will decide about the scratch on your photo. Maybe she will think that you want to have the same adorable scar? ... Don't joke with such things!

7. Someone once wrote in a book that to create collages you need to take pictures and photographs from magazines. And I did not write about the opportunity to search for a dream photo on the Internet. Maybe this author was not very friendly with the Internet, maybe he took it for granted that since you can take from magazines, you can also take from the Internet. But this phrase about photos from magazines now wanders through dozens and hundreds of sources, confusing people and adding difficulties to them when creating collages.

Therefore, we emphasize the following: there are no obstacles to using photos from the Internet when creating Treasure Maps and Dream Collages. Clear and high quality, of course.

In our opinion, working with photos from the Internet is much more convenient than fiddling with magazines. After all, you need to find magazines somewhere else, and you need to buy them. If you accidentally spoil a photo when cutting out, you won't fix anything. And you will never find such a magazine in which there would be suitable photos for all your desires. And on the Internet there are hundreds of millions of photos of any size, color, layout.

DREAM CARD - WHEN IS THE BEST TO DO

As you know, the term Dream Card has several synonyms: Treasure Card, Desires, Feng Shui, Happiness, ... Personally, we like the Dream Card and Treasure Card options more. In the materials of the site, the words Map of Dreams, Map, Map of Dreams (Treasures) mean the same thing.

Oddly enough, it is desirable to create a Dream Map in a certain period of time. Although what is really strange here, because we are talking about an almost magical artifact. Therefore, when deciding how to make this artifact, carefully consider the dates of the creation of the Map.

As is often the case, there are quite a few opinions about which periods are favorable for this. Someone says that you need to focus on the phases of the moon and lunar day, someone considers the period from Catholic Christmas to Orthodox Christmas to be the best time, many are sure that the best time is the first two weeks of the New Year according to the lunar calendar (at the same time Chinese New Year). There are a lot of opinions, and each of them has a right to exist.

We have specially studied this issue, including referring to our information Sources from the Subtle World, and now we can confidently assert that the most favorable period for creating the Map is the first 14 days of the New Year according to the lunar calendar.

Why is this particular time considered the most favorable? What is its peculiarity? In order to understand this, we need to plunge into Chinese culture and their traditions for a short while.

In China, it is believed that at this time the souls of deceased ancestors descend to Earth, and for two weeks they wander next to people, visit their descendants. In other words, at this time our physical world comes into contact with the Subtle World. It is quite natural to believe that the wishes made at such a time have a much greater chance of being fulfilled, because the action of the Dream Card (Treasure) is very similar to magic, and during this period magic is close to us as never before.

But that's not all. It is believed that even the Gods themselves descend from Heaven at this time. They roam the Earth, look into every house, to every person, and fulfill their desires and dreams.

All this Magic ends on the fifteenth day of the year, the holiday of Lanterns. On this day, millions of lanterns are lit all over the country, which, according to legend, escort the souls of ancestors to another world, who descended to earth to their loved ones. The gods also leave the Earth and go back to Heaven to quickly begin to fulfill the wishes they have collected.

Knowing all this, the Chinese devote the first fifteen days of the New Year to prayers and various rituals. They set goals, make wishes, ask for help. And not a single request made during this period remains unnoticed by the Higher Forces, because they are next to you, and your words reach them much faster.

Someone may consider all of the above to be beautiful fairy tales, but our information sources claim that this period is truly a magical time. That is why we strongly recommend making a Dream Card during this period.

The Chinese calendar does not have a fixed start date for the new year, because it depends on the phases of the moon. Because of this, the most favorable period for creating a Map is constantly shifting in time. We'll have to open the Chinese calendar, where you can find all the information you need.

The Wish Card for the year is made on the Lunar New Year or on your birthday. These are the two strongest days of the year when you can create the most working Wish Card.

Here are the upcoming Lunar New Year dates:
12 February 2021
February 1, 2022
January 22, 2023

Also, do not forget that the Wish Card for the year can be made on your birthday. This is your personal New Year and a very magical and powerful time.

The question "how to make a Dream (Treasure) Map" is perhaps one of the most frequently asked. A lot of controversy is caused by the size and frame. On numerous forums, people are happy to share their opinions on this matter, and, unfortunately, they often give absolutely wrong recommendations.

One of the most common questions is whether it is necessary to frame the Map. Most often, we give an affirmative answer to this question, because it is the frame that gives your work a complete look. In the frame The map looks beautiful and aesthetically pleasing. In addition, it will keep better in the frame. Plus, you won't damage your dreams with tape or glue.

Judge for yourself: if you hang the Map without a frame, then almost the only option to fix it on the wall is to use scotch tape, and since the Map is completely filled, the tape will inevitably lie on top of some desires, which is very bad. You can, of course, think about double-sided tape, but this option has its drawbacks.

Of course, it's best to create a frame for the Map. Of course, with glass!

CASE FROM PRACTICE

The young man made a Dream (Treasure) Map,
but decided to do without a frame, so he took and
simply stuck the Map with adhesive tape to the
wall. At the same time, in one place, the adhesive
tape was stretched over the image of the car.
The card worked great: less than a year later, the
young man bought a car. But one day he comes
to visit us, and his whole hood is dented and
wrapped in the same place and in exactly the
same adhesive tape as on the Map. Immediately
after repairing the car, the guy bought a frame for
his magic assistant ...

We strongly recommend using a frame if, of course, you decide to hang the Map on the wall. At the same time, we advise you not to skimp on your dreams, and do not try to rivet a frame from the fragments of fruit boxes. It is more correct to make a good, beautiful frame to order, which will delight the eye and serve for many years.

Surprisingly, during the magical period, there is a real boom in framing shops in some cities. For example, as soon as one of our Minsk clients crossed the threshold of such a workshop, the receptionist immediately asked, "You must be 68 to 68 for the Treasure Map? Today you are already the eighth person who orders this. "

Now we are smoothly moving on to dimensions. The question "how big to make a Treasure Map" is perhaps one of the most frequently asked questions. On numerous forums, people are happy to share their opinions on this matter, and, unfortunately, they often give absolutely wrong recommendations.

For example, some argue that the Map can be absolutely any size, but such an answer is simply impossible to hear from a professional. To use "any" size is a risk. Risk that the Card will not receive the power it could get, and even that the wrong size will reduce its effectiveness. Any competent expert knows that size matters, and that there are a number of sizes in nature that are not only undesirable, but even dangerous.

Some people think that the most remarkable size for a Map is 68 x 68 cm. This is a really beautiful option, and we have nothing against it. But it is no better than, for example, options 67 x 67 or 69 x 69 or 88 x 88 cm.

These are all quite good sizes, but before deciding to use them, decide what size paper you will use to create the Dream Map. If, for example, you want to design each Sector in Photoshop and then print on a separate A4 sheet, then the above dimensions will hardly suit you, because the maximum possible width of each sector is about 21 cm (the exact value depends on the printer model). As you remember, the A4 sheet is exactly 21 cm wide, and you also need to leave a small distance on the margins. The map consists of three sectors in height and three in width, it turns out that the maximum possible size of such a Map (without a frame) is about 63 cm. Whether it will be possible to make such a frame in order to get the desired 68 cm - you know better.

To find out which sizes are favorable and which are not, in our author's course we consider the topic of the so-called imperial sizes. In addition, the course contains a lot of other tips and subtleties on how to make the Map correctly. Now we will not talk about this, but just offer some good size options.

We have already talked about the well-known favorable options for sizes 68 x 68, 69 x 69, 88 x 88.

Here are some other very good options:
•Between 63.3 and 64.3 cm.
•Between 20.3 and 21.3 cm (this good size is also useful for creating sectors).
•between 47 and 48.2 cm.
•between 41.8 and 42.8 cm.

As a bonus, let me give you some important advice:

If you are not going to have a child yet, then you should not use the sizes of the Sectors or the Map that fall in the interval from 16.1 cm to 17.5 cm and from 59 cm to 60.5 cm. Why this is so, we will not discuss. Just take our word for it.

A little more about the frames. Our author's course provides exclusive information on what color is better to make frames and from what material in order to further increase the efficiency of the COP.

We figured out the dimensions. It remains to answer a very important question: "If the Card is inserted into a frame, then its dimensions are the dimensions of the frame or whatman paper?"

We answer: the Card inserted into the frame forms a single whole with the frame. Therefore, its dimensions are the outer dimensions of the frame.

This is a very important note! It turns out that you first need to select (or make) a frame of a favorable size, then measure with a ruler what size of the Map it includes, and only after that proceed to the fascinating lesson of drawing squares and coloring them.

Just in case. it should be mentioned that all sorts of errors can be made in the manufacture of the frame. Therefore, we advise you to draw the manufacturer's attention to the fact that the accuracy of the outer dimensions is very important.

LET'S START CREATING A WISH MAP (TREASURE OR DREAM)!

The first thing we do is draw a square of the desired size on a sheet of Whatman paper. Surely you have already prepared a beautiful frame with glass, so you know exactly what size the sheet will fit into it. We draw a square of this size. Then we divide the drawn square into 9 more identical squares. These actions are simple, but very important, because they are the official beginning of the creation of the Map.

In many cases, it is impossible to accurately divide a large square into nine absolutely equal squares, because some sizes simply cannot be divisible by three without a remainder. For example, if you take the beloved by many size 68 x 68, it turns out that each of the nine squares should be 22.6666666 x 22.6666666. But it doesn't matter. It is not at all scary if one square differs by a couple of millimeters from the second, or if the width and height of some square slightly coincide. The main thing is that visually all the squares look the same.

Of course, this only applies to small errors of one or two millimeters, which will be completely invisible. If the difference in size is obvious, then everything will have to be redone.

If you make a Map in Photoshop, it will be easier to work with each square separately, so you just create them and save each one under your own name. Be sure to make sure all squares are the same size and resolution.

Coloring the squares

After the large square is carefully drawn and carefully divided into 9 small squares, the fun begins - all the squares need to be painted in different colors. For many people, it is the coloring process that gives the greatest pleasure. Well, when can grown up uncles and aunts take up paints and feel like children again?

Note that it is not at all necessary to use paints, instead of them you can use colored paper, or print multi-colored squares on a color printer. If you will do the whole Dream Map in Photoshop, then simply fill the background of each of the squares with the necessary color without printing them. It should only be taken into account that the colors on the display screen can be very strikingly different from the colors that will be obtained when printed on a printer. Therefore, it will be very prudent to make sure in advance that the print result is satisfactory. Try to first print samples of all the colors that will be used to fill the squares and make sure they match the required ones.

Let's go back to coloring the squares. Even in such a simple matter there are very important nuances. First, each square must be of a strictly defined color. It is absolutely impossible to violate the color scheme, because if at least one square is of the "wrong" color, then your magic tool may stop working altogether.

The colors of the squares are as follows:

south (upper square) - red,
north (lower) - blue,
west (right) - white
east (left) - green

southeast (upper left) - light green or light green,
southwest (upper right) brown,
north - west (bottom right) - gray,
 northeast (bottom left) - light brown,
central - yellow.

Let us remind you an important advice: if you understand that for some reason you cannot paint some squares in the desired colors, then paint the entire Map in one color. It's better than breaking her color scheme.

As a result, you will have something like this structure.

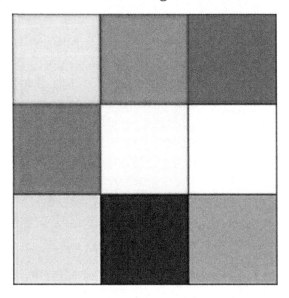

Fig. 1 Dream Map, color of sectors

After you have painted the squares, it is advisable to call them not squares, but respectfully - Sectors. That's right - with a capital letter.

Filling Sectors

Now it remains to place photo collages in each of the Sectors that correspond to one or another of your dreams. Surely you have already made a Dream Collage for yourself, so you can imagine how it should look.

It is when filling the Sectors that people make the maximum number of mistakes. For example, many for some reason try to fill all Sectors at the same time. We saw a suitable photo of a beautiful car - and immediately pasted it into the Wealth Sector. The next step is to stick a picture of Paris into the Travel Sector so that it does not get lost, and immediately take the image of a couple in love and place it in the Love Sector. Such random throwing from one Sector to another and back is one of the most serious mistakes, which can significantly reduce the effectiveness of the Map.

Sectors should be filled in one by one. This is exactly what our Information Sources advise.

Where does this demand come from? Probably, the point is this: if we constantly jump from one Sector to another, from one group of desires to the second and to the third, then we cannot concentrate on each of the desires. My head is full of confusion about a car, the Eiffel Tower, a wedding, a new position and so on. In addition, there will be a constant return to the previous Sectors: "Ah, I completely forgot that I also want to lose weight." As a result, awareness of the choice of the main goals is lost, there is no concentration on them. The main idea that a person possesses is to place pictures more beautifully and hang up a map as soon as possible. The world is at a loss - it cannot understand what we really want.

When we design each Sector from start to finish, we carefully analyze our desires in advance and select the most important of them. Therefore, we know exactly what we want to place in one or another Sector. This will be exactly what is most important to us. And when we start filling the Sector, then all our thoughts will be only about this area of life, only about this desire. We post a picture of our own wedding and at the same time clearly imagine the admiring glances of others. We work with a photo of a car and clearly see ourselves behind the wheel of a brand new car, we inhale the factory smells of the interior. In this case, the Energy of our dreams transferred to the Card will be much stronger. Of course, the World understands much more clearly what exactly we want, therefore it will be able to help the fulfillment of our plans much more effectively.

This is also why we advised you to think in advance what exactly you want to portray in a particular Sector.

There is one more very important rule, all the Squares must be filled! It is categorically impossible to leave empty, even filled-in Squares! If, for example, you cannot think of any desires to fill the Knowledge Sector with (although it is quite easy to come up with something for this Sector!), Then picture yourself reading a book or watching TV.

Let us recall what each of the 9 Sectors is responsible for.

Fig. 2 Sectors of the Dream Map (Treasure)

We decorate with beads

Finally, all the Sectors are completed. The final touch remains. We frame each Sector of the Card around the perimeter with a narrow strip of beads, several beads wide. It is imperative that the beads match the color of the corresponding Sector. Of course, you do not need to try to achieve an exact match of the shade, and this is impossible. If, for example, your Travel Sector is light gray, and, as luck would have it, there are only dark gray beads, nothing bad will happen. Moreover, the difference between the shade of the main color of the Square and the shade of the beads will further decorate your magic assistant. The beads will match the Square, and it is so beautiful!

Why do all this? There are several reasons for this. Firstly, the joints of the various Squares should not be visible, and the strips of beads mask these joints. This is a very important argument. Please note that this requirement also applies to those Maps whose Squares are painted by hand, which makes the joints of two multi-colored Squares uneven, and those Maps that are drawn perfectly in Photoshop.

The second reason is that beads are some kind of jewelry, wealth, beauty, etc. Thus, it enhances the work of our magic instrument.

Apparently, there are other reasons, we just haven't figured them out yet. It's not that important. It is quite enough that our Sources of Information consider the use of beads as one of the fundamental rules when working with the Card. Note that we rarely used such expressions in the course. Therefore, we repeat once again: the edging of the Map Sectors with beads is extremely desirable!

This rule applies to all versions of the **Wish Map**. And those that will hang on the wall, and those that will live in folders or albums.

Probably, there may be situations when the edging of the Squares is impossible for one reason or another. Well, then the Dream Card won't get very significant support. At the same time, it is absolutely obvious that it is much better to have a Map without a Sector border than not to have it at all. This should be the starting point.

Let's make a reservation that you can use not only beads for edging, but other materials as well. For example, powder for nail design with sparkles, or precious and semi-precious stones, or Swarovski crystals, or even diamonds ... Perhaps the most afford-able and successful option is still beads.

Please note that it is strictly not allowed to use something broken, broken, etc. That is, the option of finely crushing glass Christmas tree decorations is absolutely not suitable. Perhaps in beauty it will be better than beads, but in terms of the applied En-ergy it will not suit absolutely.

The figure below shows schematically how the Sectors are fram-ing. To make the picture clearer, we had to specifically desaturate all the Sectors, but you know that all nine Sectors are painted over!

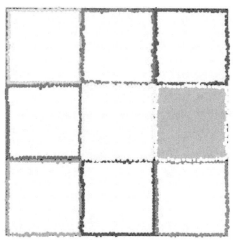

Fig 3. Edging the Sectors of the Dream Map

Moreover, to show the edging of the right middle Sector with white beads, we had to paint over it with gray, otherwise the white beads on white would be indistinguishable. But you know that this is the White Sector!

Edging the Sector is very simple, you need to apply a narrow strip of glue 5-10 mm wide around the perimeter of each Square, and sprinkle the beads on top and give it a little time to stick. Then tilt the Card and the excess beads will fall off it.

It is even more convenient to string the beads on a thread (fishing line) of the required length, and then stick them around the Sector. Perhaps two or three parallel strings will look more beautiful than one.

Important! The previous picture shows that each Sector is framed with beads on all 4 sides. But in practice, this may prevent you from accurately inserting the sheet with the Card into the prepared frame. Therefore, it is possible not to use beads on those sides of the Sectors that are in contact with the frame.

Only now the Map can be considered ready. It remains to place it in a frame, and hang it on the wall at an opportune moment.

PLACES OF DESIRES ON THE MAP OF DESIRES (WISH BOARD)

We've all heard (at least most of us :)) that like attracts like! So, for example, if we want money in the wallet, then we put a certain bill in the wallet as a bait or magnet. If we want to find a soul mate, then we surround ourselves with symbols of love, etc.

The same thing happens with the Treasure Map! It is not without reason that we not only write the formulation of our desire, but also place its image on the Map. And we also add certain amplifiers to each Sector of the Treasure Map to further activate the execution of our plans.

It is important to remember and understand that everything on the Map is not accidental! And for a reason, we advise you to keep the desired income in your hands in the Wealth Sector, place all the elements in pairs in the Love Sector, and not to put the child's image in the Children and Creativity Sector if you do not plan to become parents in the coming year :)

There is one more secret, which we have not yet talked about, but decided to share with you today! And it belongs to the Treasure Map Travel and Assistants Sector!

As a rule, most of the people who create the Treasure Map place in this Sector an image of the country (and some even several :)), in which they dream of rest. And as a rule, in every country there are magical places (and in some, more than one :)), where you can make wishes!

By placing in the Travel Sector not just an image of the country you want to visit, but an image of such a magical place, you will additionally activate your Treasure Map (online wish board) and give it even more magic!

So, among the endless number of Magic Places, we have selected ten that you can place on your Treasure Map (download wish board). Here you can find pictures for your wish board for free:

1. Israel. Western Wall in Jerusalem.
The Wailing Wall is a sacred place for all Jews. In the crack of the wall, you must put a piece of paper on which the desire is written. It is believed that in this way the note gets to God.

2. Egypt. Statue of the sacred scarab beetle in Luxor.
The stone figure of the Beetle is located on a column near the temple of Amun on the territory of the Karnak complex. It is ne-

cessary to go around the column seven times counterclockwise for the plan to come true.

3. Turkey. House of the Virgin Mary in Ephesus.

As you know, it was in Ephesus that the Virgin Mary spent the rest of her life. This sacred place is regularly visited by pilgrims and tourists. Here you can light candles, collect holy water in the springs, and you can leave your wishes on the wall next to the house.

4. Bulgaria. The bridge of desires in Varna.

If you go to the indicated Bridge in the Sea Garden of the city of Varna with your eyes closed and make a wish, then it will definitely come true. There was once a small pond under the bridge, into which couples in love threw coins. It was believed that after that, their love would last longer.

5. France. Eiffel Tower in Paris.

Paris itself is a magical city. The city of love, the city of creativity ... In Paris you can find many magical places, but we decided to stop at the symbol of this city - the Eiffel Tower. The tower has a pyramidal shape, but the pyramids are directly connected with the Cosmos, which means that if you make a wish while standing directly under the tower, it will be delivered to the exact address :)

6. Czech Republic. Charles Bridge in Prague.

This bridge is a visiting card of the Czech Republic, one of the most beautiful in Europe and, according to the legend, the date of the beginning of the construction of the bridge was determined by astrologers! Feel free to dream in this magical place and everything will come true!

7. Belgium. Bas-relief of St. Michael and his dog in Brussels.

You can see this bas-relief in the arch located on the main square of the city. To make your plan come true, you need to stroke the saint and the dog's head without lifting your hands.

8. Italy. Trevi Fountain in Rome.
It is the largest and most famous fountain in Rome. Coins thrown into the fountain contribute to finding happiness in your personal life!

9. Greece. Valley of the seven streams on the island of Rhodes.
After making your most cherished wish and repeating it like a mantra, walk barefoot through the icy water along a 186-meter tunnel to a mountain lake, into which numerous springs run down. After passing this test, your wish will come true!

10. India. Delhi post.
In order for the wish to come true, it is necessary to stand with your back to the column, wrap your arms around it and stand in this position for several minutes. According to local residents, the pillar also promotes healing from diseases and brings happiness.

But remember that for the fulfillment of desires, one Treasure Map (creating a wish board), even if with an image of a place that contributes to the fulfillment of the desired, is not enough. We also need your active actions in the right direction!

WHERE TO HANG THE DREAM CARD

One of the most frequent questions that we are asked is where to hang the finished Dream (Treasure) Card. As you can imagine, we are now talking about the large size options, and not about the ones that were specially sized to fit in a folder or wallet.

For large Maps, there is an important rule: it must hang. That's when she works to the maximum. We've seen a large Treasure Map just sit on the floor, leaning against a wall, under a bed, or on a cupboard. Subsequent study of the state of such specimens led to very sad conclusions: they stopped working, offended by disrespect.

The best Dream Card is the one that hangs!

Traditionally, the best locations for the Map are east and southeast, and we generally agree with this opinion. It would be nice, of course, to calculate the number of Gua for the creator of the Map, and select the direction based on this, but this is already somewhat more difficult. Therefore, the above directions are quite suitable: east and southeast.

And this is where the problems begin. Many people make colossal mistakes by thoughtlessly following the east-southeast recommendation. They don't even think about the fact that placing the Map in some places could offend her.

Therefore, we consider it necessary to emphasize the following: even if the chosen direction for placement is not entirely successful, then a catastrophe will not occur, the efficiency of work will not decrease, there will simply not be an additional increase in its efficiency.

But if you try at any cost to choose the most favorable (from the point of view of all the recommended direction) wall, then it is quite possible to get a non-working Map. To avoid getting into a similar situation, check out our recommendations.

The best places for placement are the living room, study and bedroom. So try to use them first.

You should not hang your magic assistant on the wall, on the other side of which there is a toilet, bathroom or kitchen. The problem is not at all that water flows in these places and all desires will be "washed off into the sewer". It's just that from the point of view of energy, the toilet and bathroom are the most unfavorable rooms in the house, because these are places for draining waste and cleaning it from dirt. The kitchen is not so bad in this regard, but if possible, avoid using the wall on the other side of which the kitchen is located. Of course, for the same reasons, placement inside a bathroom, toilet, closet or kitchen should not be considered. Don't risk it! We have faced situations where the Map placed in the bathroom simply refused to work.

The corridor is also not the best place. Although the layouts are now the most sophisticated, and it is quite possible that it is in your apartment that the corridor has a charming nook near the bedroom, almost closed from prying eyes.

The Map should not be placed on the window.

The Pantry is not a place for a Dream Card! The map is in no way like temporarily unnecessary things!

Placing the Map in a closet packed with rags is also a very controversial idea. She's alive! And you put her in the closet!

One of the most frequent questions is whether the Map can be placed where outsiders can see it. The decision depends on several factors, incl. on how close these people are to you and how shy you are. All people are different, some keep their desires deep inside, while others calmly talk about them with others.

We believe that the Dream Map should be hidden from the eyes of those who are not included in the circle of people closest to a person. Shyness isn't the only problem. Such an unusual artifact will attract the attention of others and evoke a variety of thoughts. It seems that many of these thoughts will be negative (as often happens when people are faced with something strange), and only a few people will be able to treat the Card positively. But negative thoughts and emotions of others are quite capable of reducing its effectiveness.

Imagine that Karta caught the eye of a man who is cynical, rude, stupid, envious and, moreover, does not believe in the possibility of miracles. Obviously, one should not expect anything good from such a spectator, only ridicule, disdain, envy and stories to everyone he meets, transverse about what he saw. These negative emotions and Energies will obviously not be of benefit to your magic assistant.

There is one more argument for not putting the Card on public display: there is no need for others to know about your innermost desires. In addition, there is a good rule: "If you dream about something, then do not tell everyone about your dream."

But if your closest friend herself has been creating her Dream Map for several years, and if she is aware of your most intimate secrets, then we do not see anything dangerous in the fact that she will see yours. If you are loved and understood at home, you don't have to hide the Map.

How can you hide the Map from unwanted eyes? It's not that hard. You can just take it off before the arrival of not the closest people, and then return it to the place. Just do not forget, while temporarily removing the Map, to explain to her what and why you are doing ...

One of our acquaintances did even more interesting: she hung her Map in a niche in the wall and designed this niche as a window with curtains. When everyone is at home, the window is open. When guests arrive, the curtains close.

CORRECT ACTIVATION OF THE CARD. HOW TO MAKE A TREASURE MAP

So, your Treasure Map is already fully prepared and framed. It remains to hang it in a pre-selected place and admire it.

The moment when we hang the Card on the wall is very, very, very important, its effectiveness and how quickly our desires will be fulfilled depends on it. Therefore, it is very important to carry out the activation correctly, following all the conditions and recommendations.

Firstly, we ONLY hang the Card on a good day and a good time! (You can find them out from our newsletters).

Secondly, we must have a good mood and a positive attitude.

You are now working with the Subtle World, therefore negative emotions are unacceptable. They will be recorded in the Map, and all work can go down the drain. If you are in a bad mood, it is better to postpone the activation until the next good date.

Thirdly, you cannot hang up the Treasure Map in a hurry, or doing several things in parallel. The card is a touchy creature. Although, it would be more correct to say otherwise: she understands her importance and requires an appropriate respectful attitude towards herself. If you simultaneously cook semolina porridge and hang the Card, then she may well think that porridge is more important for you. With all the ensuing consequences.

In addition, we strongly recommend conducting a small and uncomplicated Treasure Map activation ritual. Ritual is almost always good. As aptly noted in one of the Kryon books, "Spirit loves rituals" (the term Spirit here means God, Absolute, Peace, etc.). Rituals give a person confidence in success ("if carrying out a certain ritual helps thousands of people, it will help me too"). Rituals help a person concentrate on an important action, and not be torn between him and porridge.

Treasure Map Activation Ritual

If the Map was made for the family, then it would be good if everyone who created it and for whom it was made would participate in the ritual. If not everyone treats this process in a properly respectful way, then it would be better to send them to the store for bread.

Now let's move on to the ritual. One should not be afraid of the word ritual. This is not necessarily something complicated, requiring, for example, some freshly dried mice and dried snakes.

So let's get started.

About 20-30 minutes before the desired time, transfer the Treasure Map to the room where it will hang. Disconnect mobile phones, TV, computer. Ventilate the room.

Take a shower and then put on something new. New underwear or socks are fine.

It is best to dress in light, loose clothing. It should be simple and beautiful at the same time. It is not necessary to carry out the ritual in a dressing gown, which has long been decorated with picturesque spots awaiting the arrival of advertisers of washing powder.

Play some calm, relaxing music. Surely you have at home some kind of disc from the series "For relaxation", "For meditation". Try to relax, disconnect for a while from all mundane activities. Take a few deep breaths, mentally count from one hundred to one.

Gently take the frame, hold it in weight, peering at the Map. Perhaps you will be able to feel some Energies coming from the awakening Treasure Map.

Hang her slowly in the place where she will live. Of course, the hook is pre-installed in this place.

Now sit comfortably in front of the Map so that you can clearly see all the Sectors and all its details. You can sit down, lie down, or continue to stand. You need to go through each desire and imagine that it has come true. Do not hurry. Feel your joy, your delight at this moment. Thank the World for making this wish come true. We do it according to all desires. Having passed all the desires of one Sector, we move on to another and so on to the end.

Finally, thank the Card again.

That's it, the ritual is over.

If you created your Card not for wall placement, but in A4 format or for a wallet, then the ritual changes a little. Instead of hanging it on the wall, you place it in a folder or some other place and then start an exciting journey according to your desires and dreams.

WHAT TO DO AFTER CREATING A MAP

Finally, the Treasure Map is hung on the wall or placed in a folder, album, wallet. So, what is next? What to do with it?

How to behave

Maybe it would be right to just forget about the existence of such? Or, on the contrary, to sit all day long, staring at her? Neither one nor the other.

You don't need to "get hung up" on the Map and your desires. If you constantly think "when will everything come true?", "Where are you, my white car", etc., then there will be no sense. There is no need to be like that donkey from the cartoon about Shrek, which every few minutes asked: "Have you arrived yet?" No need to pull the World. Everyone knows for themselves how difficult it is to do something when they are constantly distracted with stupid questions. So let go of the situation, do not focus on it. Let the World work in peace.

But forgetting about your Magic Promoter will also be wrong. She is almost alive, we have already talked about this, and she will be very offended by inattention. You need to work with her: watch, you can even talk. Visualize the fulfillment of those desires that are placed on the Map. There are many of them, so do not try to imagine the fulfillment of all desires at once. Be sure to thank both the Card and the World for fulfilling your next wish.

Do not part with the Card so that it does not feel unnecessary to you. If you are leaving somewhere, then take a small photo and put it in your wallet, for example. Or print it at a reduced scale for this. Now you will be together even far from each other.

If you change your place of residence, it goes without saying that the Card will move with you.

And most importantly, take action.

The World has no hands but yours. Even if the World decides that you are worthy of a huge lottery win, you will have to buy a ticket.

The world can only provide opportunities, and only you can take advantage of them. And remember that the world can once cre-ate the conditions for the fulfillment of a dream, the second, the third ... But if you are lying on the couch and are not going to take advantage of these opportunities, then the next time may not be. What is the point for the Map and the World to try if you don't need it!

HOW TO CHANGE
THE TREASURE MAP

The question "how to change the Treasure Map" says only one thing - the person did not take a very responsible approach to its creation - he did not carefully think over all desires.

Some authors confidently recommend removing already come true wishes from the Map and placing new ones instead. We have specially studied this issue, consulted with our sources from the Subtle World and categorically do not recommend making any changes after activation - this is very, very unfavorable!

You can easily replace the Dream Collage with a new one, but the Treasure Map is a completely different matter!

This technique is a holistic mechanism that triggers positive changes in almost all areas of your life. And after activation, there is a kind of planning of actions for all your desires, and these actions for one desires are interconnected with work on others. As a result, a certain program is created to realize all the wishes of the Card. Then this program starts up, gains strength and begins to be implemented.

Now imagine that after the fulfillment of some desires, you place new ones.

First, it will be a different Map. She needs time to start working.

Secondly, it will again be necessary to create programs for the realization of desires, taking into account the newly emerged ones, and this is a serious waste of time. As a result, your Magic Tool will spend most of the time creating new programs and launching them, and not systematically working on the realization of desires.

Imagine a car racing. The car picking up speed rushes along the highway. Nothing seems to stop her. But suddenly a command appears - to enter the box. We will change something. Then again acceleration, set of speed, and again the team - into boxing. And so it is constantly. Do you think this car will be able to win?

In addition, constantly changing desires, you are trying to turn the Card into your servant, into Cinderella. Did you complete this task? Then fulfill this desire. And now this. So what if we did not agree on this when creating it, I want-want-want....

Therefore, think three times whether it really is necessary to make any changes. In most cases, it turns out that this is not at all necessary.

Perhaps we can imagine the one and only case when correction is really necessary - the presence of a photograph of a person who began to cause negative feelings. This can happen, for example, if, in violation of all our recommendations, a photo of a particular person is placed in the upper right Sector (Love, Relationships). Anything can happen in a year, including the final breakdown of relations, and betrayal and betrayal ... Once at a time it does not happen, but someone's negative emotions that arise when they see this person on the Map can be so strong that a complete blockage is possible Cards. In such a situation, there is no way out, you need to take a photo.

What to do in a year with the Treasure Map

A year has passed, you are already working on a new Card. And what to do with the old one?

When it comes time to create a new Map, you should wholeheartedly thank last year for everything she helped, for her work. We recommend taking a photo of the Card as a keep-sake. Then take it out of the frame and cut it into small - small pieces that are best burned. If it is impossible to burn, then put the "noodles" obtained after cutting the Card in a black bag and take it to the trash can.

All actions to liquidate the old Card should be done with due respect to it.

None of its elements can be used categorically when creating a new one. Even if some desires did not come true, and you want to place them on a new Map, then these goals need to be formalized again.

The strict recommendation not to use anything from the old Card is easy to explain: all its elements are filled with Energy with the deadline for fulfilling desires that has already expired. This means that not only will they not work on the new Treasure Map, but they will also interfere with the fulfillment of new desires, transferring their own "last year" Energy to them.

WHY THE CARD
MAY NOT WORK

There is such a situation: the Treasure Map is created, but time passes, and almost nothing comes true. Why? The simplest (but not necessarily the most correct) answer comes to mind first: "Because a mistake was made when creating it." Indeed, there are many nuances and details that are highly undesirable to neglect. Therefore, it is quite possible to assume that the totality of the mistakes made sharply reduced the efficiency of this tool.

But it would be a big foolishness to look for the reason for the poor performance of the Map only in errors during its creation! Judge for yourself: the simplest Dream Collage, made without any understanding of the rules at all, can have amazing results. Now we are considering a possible situation where a much more powerful technique does not work. In such a situation, it is necessary to analyze not so much the mistakes made during its creation, as the actions, thoughts and emotions of the creator himself.

It is clear that it is useless to wait from the Map of Miracles if, after its creation, a person falls on the sofa and spends all his time there. Then nothing in life will change, no dreams will come true. Judge for yourself: even if the World is ready to help you win the lottery, you will first need to get off the couch and buy a ticket. If the world is ready to help you meet your love, then it would be nice to think about your appearance, otherwise weekly stubble and leaky dirty socks can ruin the girl's first impression. And to make your dream come true to relax in the Bahamas, you will have to issue a passport in advance.

The world can provide opportunities, but only you can take advantage of them. And remember that the World can once create conditions for the fulfillment of a dream, the second, the third ... And the next time may not be, if you have not tried to use the previous opportunities. What is the point for the World to try if you don't need it!

Now let's talk about the influence of a person's actions, thoughts, emotions on the effectiveness of this magical tool. Almost nobody mentions this.

Let's ask a provocative question: will even a perfectly made Treasure Map work for a criminal who goes out to rob old women every night? The obvious answer is no! After all, the map does not work by itself, it is a part of the World, as, indeed, does each of us. She uses the support of the World and therefore works effectively when the World is ready to help the creator of the Map.

One of the three fundamental Laws of our World is the Law of the Supremacy of Love: the most important and valuable thing in our World is Love. The world appreciates and supports precisely Love and good, not hatred and evil. A person who robbing old women brings evil, not love. Of course, he will not receive support from the World.

It turns out that the degree to which the World helps each of us to a great extent depends on how correctly we behave, what actions we do, what emotions we experience, what thoughts wander in our heads. For example, if someone considers the World to be hostile, then the World will not dissuade them from this, therefore no miracles will be created. Simplifying, we can say that it is not the World that first has to prove that it is "good" by giving you to win the lottery, but on the contrary - you first need to treat the World with love, and then it will start helping.

Many people completely mistakenly believe that only actions can interfere with the fulfillment of desires. This is absolutely wrong. Negative thoughts and emotions have a huge impact. For example, even as a joke, without any evil, the said phrase "if you do not do it in time - I will kill" has great consequences. If a person is filled with anger, irritability, aggression, if he sees bad in everything, then he can hardly count on the help of the World.

Therefore, take a closer look at yourself, at your actions, thoughts, emotions, at your attitude towards the people around you, and start working to ensure that the World helps you with more and more pleasure. Constantly change for the better. The discussion of how to do this is outside the scope of our site. We can only advise, for example, to carefully study the literature on the system of positive thinking. This is a very good system, we assure you!

Another fairly common reason for the "inoperability" of the Card is the wrong attitude towards it.

She's almost alive, she can be very offended by inattention to herself. And she will not tolerate if a person perceives it in the same way as a soulless TV remote control, which should produce exactly the result that corresponds to the pressed button.

We have now discussed not all the reasons why the Treasure Map may not work as we would like. But these are perhaps the most important reasons.

DOES THE TREASURE MAP GUARANTEE THE DESIRED OUTCOME?

When talking about a method or method, it is customary to report guarantees. many are looking for reviews of the wish card (dreams). If you recently bought some kind of equipment or computer programs, then for sure remember the long texts, which describe in detail the guarantees and those cases when the guarantee does not apply.

And in the case of the Treasure Map, a long text is not required, because there are no guarantees at all that your wishes and dreams will come true. Surely, you yourself understand why this is so, but we will nevertheless repeat the main theses.

There are no ways in the world that can guarantee the achievement of any goals for any person. There are no people in the world who would be able to solve any problem of any person. Why? Because EVERYTHING that happens to a person, he himself created. This is one of the basic Laws of our World: a person himself forms all the events of his life.

The bad news: whether your dreams come true or not, depends only on you.

The good news: whether your dreams come true or not, depends only on you.

And only you decide whether this news is good or bad. In our opinion, this is not just good, but great news!

All changes in a person's life are impossible without his own active actions and without the World finding it possible to help him. Again, let's ask a rhetorical question: will the World help a person who robs old women at night?

So there is no guarantee of success.

But!

You're not going to sit back after creating a Wish (Dream) Map, are you? And you sincerely want to change internally for the better. And this means that there is a very, very high probability that the World will start, through the Treasure Map, to help you fulfill your desires and dreams. And the more you yourself change for the better, the more the World will help you.

ABOUT THE AUTHOR

Alex Magic

This amazing book was written by the great practicing feng shui master and astrologer of our time. The author is Professor of Psychology, Doctor of Astrology and Parapsychology at the London School of Astrology, Honorary Academician of the School of Traditional Medicine and Feng Shui Practice of China.

A successful astrologer of our time, author of textbooks and founder of the school of astrology and feng shui Alex Magic, where he teaches according to his own method, which has long established itself as the strongest and incredibly effective.